YOUNG ARTISTS DRAW MANGA

Christopher Hart

Watson-Guptill Publications / New York

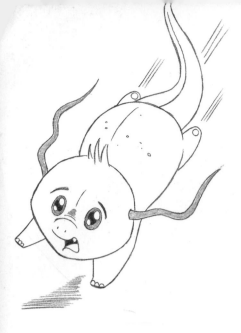

Library of Congress Cataloging-in-Publication Data
Hart, Christopher.
Young artists draw manga / Christopher Hart.—1st ed.
p. cm.
ISBN 978-0-8230-2657-9
1. Comic books, strips, etc.—Japan—Technique—Juvenile
literature. 2. Cartooning—Technique—Juvenile literature. 3. Comic
strip characters—Japan—Juvenile literature. I. Title.
NC1764.5.J3H379 2009   741.5′1—dc22
2010038311

Printed in China

Design by Karla Baker
Cover design by Jess Morphew
Front cover art by Christopher Hart

10 9 8 7 6 5 4 3 2 1

First Edition

CONTENTS

INTRODUCTION

Manga is the cartoon style from Japan that has swept the country. It is super-popular with teens and kids and is seen in graphic novels, video games, and animation, where it is known as anime (pronounced "ah-nah-may"). With just a little help from this book, you can draw all the coolest styles of manga: the big-eyed, pretty girls of shoujo; the heartthrob guys of bishounen; the adventurous heroes of shounen; plus adorable chibis, fantasy creatures, Goth characters, and more.

DRAWING BASICS

We'll start by learning some basic art principles and how they relate to drawing manga faces and bodies. The rest of the book is pure drawing fun. With less text, there's more room for the drawings. And we've stuffed this book to the brim with helpful, instructive step-by-step illustrations. In fact, there are over 125 original characters within these pages, each different and ready to inspire. So pick up a pencil, and let's get started!

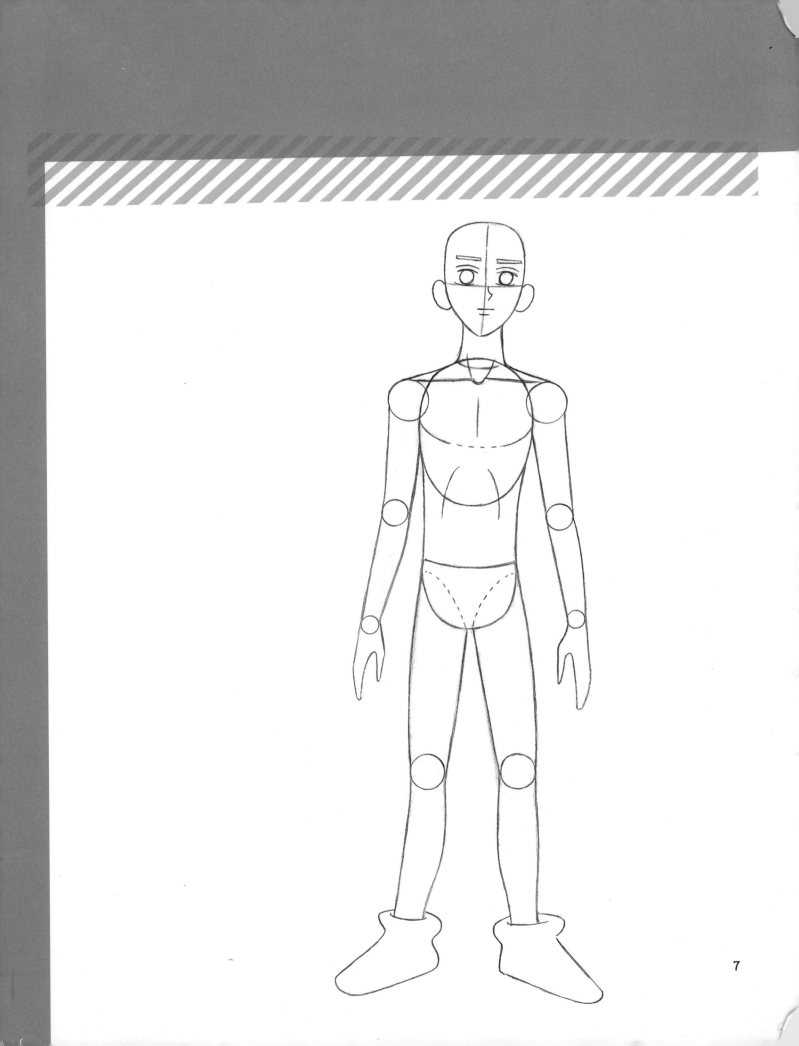

THE TONE WHEEL

The tone wheel shows all of the pencil tones you'll see in this book. You can get all of these shades from an ordinary pencil. It adds extra zing to a drawing when you vary the shading. For example, the boy in this picture has a different tone on his tie than he does on his pants, his hair is two-toned for added punch, and his pants are shaded a light gray. That's more interesting than if all his shading were the same tone of gray.

DRAWiNG THE HEAD

We use sketch lines, one vertical (up and down) and one horizontal (left to right), drawn lightly on the head, to help us place the features where they should go. That way, it won't be "hit or miss" every time we try to draw a face.

1 This is called the *center line*, and it divides the face into two equal parts. The nose is drawn near or on the center line. The eyes are both the same distance from the center line, in order to look balanced.

2 This is called the *eye line*. The eyes rest on top of this line. In manga characters, this line is placed low on the head.

3 The ears are also drawn low on the head, especially on kids and teen characters.

4 Because we have set the eye line so low, the forehead ends up large. Cover the forehead with lots of manga-style hair.

5 The low eye line also means that the mouth area and chin will be small, even petite.

DRAWING THE MANGA FACE

Boys' and girls' heads are generally the same shape, which makes them easy to draw, but boys have a slightly wider jaw and thicker neck, which makes them look a bit more masculine. The eyes are the big difference between male and female manga characters. The females are drawn with glamorous eyelashes, while the males are given heavier eyebrows. And the eyes themselves are not quite as fancy on boys as they are on girls.

1   **Another good reason to sketch the eye line before you draw the eyes: It keeps the eyes perfectly even, so they don't look lopsided, with one higher than the other.**

2   **Unless your character is making an off-center expression with his mouth, the mouth is usually centered on the center line.**

3   **Spiky hair is typical of male manga characters.**

4   **The hair flops over the forehead, another classic look for male manga characters.**

MANGA EYES

There are many ways to draw manga eyes, but most manga eyes have two large shines in them. Let's start with the standard, classic types. From these, you can create a lot of different varieties. But it's a good idea to get the standard, reliable ones down first. Try practicing these.

FEMALE

1 Draw thicker eyelashes and eyelids on top.

2 Bottom eyelid and eyelashes should be thin.

3 Bottom eyelids don't attach—they float!

4 Eyebrows should be curved, not straight.

5 Include two eye shines per pupil.

MALE

1 Manga boys have no eyelashes.

2 The eyelids are closer to the eye than those of female characters.

3 The eyebrows should be thick and can be curved or straight.

4 Eye is shaded in three tones (white, gray, and, black).

DRAWING THE MANGA BODY

Drawing the body can be complicated, so artists make it easier by breaking the body into simple shapes and then joining them together. Since anyone can draw these simple shapes—such as circles, ovals, curved, and straight lines—it makes sketching the body simpler.

FRONT VIEW—GIRL

This teen girl has idealized proportions. Let's examine the diagram and see what makes her proportions so perfect for a manga heroine.

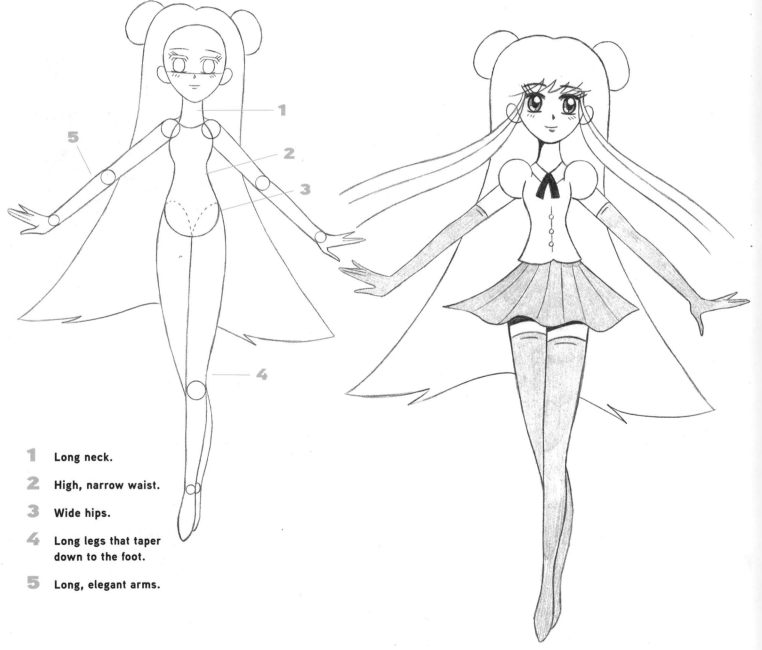

1   **Long neck.**

2   **High, narrow waist.**

3   **Wide hips.**

4   **Long legs that taper down to the foot.**

5   **Long, elegant arms.**

SiDE ViEW—GiRL

Beginners often draw the side view so that it looks too stiff, with lots of straight lines. Actually, the key to a great side view is lots of curved lines! When drawing the side view, it's important that the back is curved, while the stomach is pretty straight. And the legs are also curved, not straight lines, as most beginners draw them.

1 Curve at middle of back.

2 Straight line for stomach.

3 Pointed toes for a graceful, flying pose.

4 Shoulders back creates a more feminine pose.

13

FRONT VIEW—BOY

The chest and shoulders are wide on a boy character's frame. He's got a thin waist, but it's not nearly as narrow as the girl character's. His torso is a single shape. We add circles to the top to show the significant shoulder muscles. At the bottom of his torso is sort of a half circle, which represents the hips. Both legs should wedge into the hip area (note the dotted lines).

1 See how the shoulders have a natural slope to them?

2 A portion of the circle (shoulder) appears inside of the torso, but most of it appears outside of it.

3 The rib cage is represented by a large oval shape.

4 The hips are small on male characters.

5 The arms, when relaxed, will show that the fingertips extend about halfway down the length of the thigh.

SiDE ViEW—BOY

I've moved his arms away from his upper body so that you can see his whole physique. At this angle, you can more clearly see the ribcage (the oval that represents the upper body). Notice that the lines that connect the rib cage to the hips are curved, and not "ruler-straight."

1 This oval represents the rib cage.

2 This shape is the hip area.

3 Collarbone sticks out just a bit.

4 Chest muscles curve forward.

5 Slight bump-out for the knee.

6 Calf muscle should be curved.

DRAWiNG HANDS

The best way to learn how to draw hands is to practice drawing them from many different angles, and so I've included a bunch of hand gestures and poses for you to practice. Fists are especially important, the tricky part being the way the thumb wraps around the fist.

In most hand poses, try varying the finger placement to create interest. Although there are no hard-and-fast rules, most manga artists don't draw the fingernails. Unlike American animated cartoons, most manga comics show four fingers, not three.

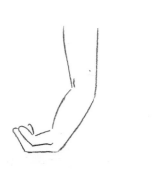

DRAWING FEET AND FOOTWEAR

If you're having some trouble drawing feet for your characters—you're not alone! Lots of beginning artists have difficulty drawing feet and shoes. Here are some hints and tips to help you.

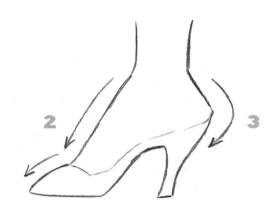

1 Pants bunch up just before they hit the sneakers.

2 There are two bumps from instep to toe on high-heeled shoes.

3 Round out the heel.

4 Notice how the inside of the foot snakes around in an S shape.

5 The inner ankle is always higher than the outer ankle.

6 The inner toe bone is always lower than the outer.

7 The big toe has a ridge and downward slope.

8 The arch of the foot is hidden in shadow.

9 Heel always bumps out.

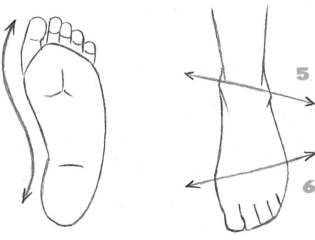

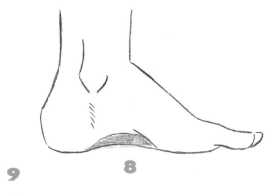

THE CHARACTERS

Now we move onto the most fun part of the book—the characters! Every finished piece of character art has six gradual steps that you can easily follow, helping you to do a great job in creating your own manga. You can copy the drawings exactly as you see them, or change little things here and there to add your own personal style and make them your own.

SHOUJO STYLE

This section introduces us to the most popular style of manga: shoujo (pronounced "show-joe"). Shoujo characters have those famous oversized glistening eyes. Their heads are large, but their features, including the nose and mouth, are small and delicate. Shoujo girl characters are often portrayed as having a charming likeability—and pretty. The boys are good-natured.

Caring Teen Girl

Pretty Girl with Glasses

Walking Home

Sweet Sixteen

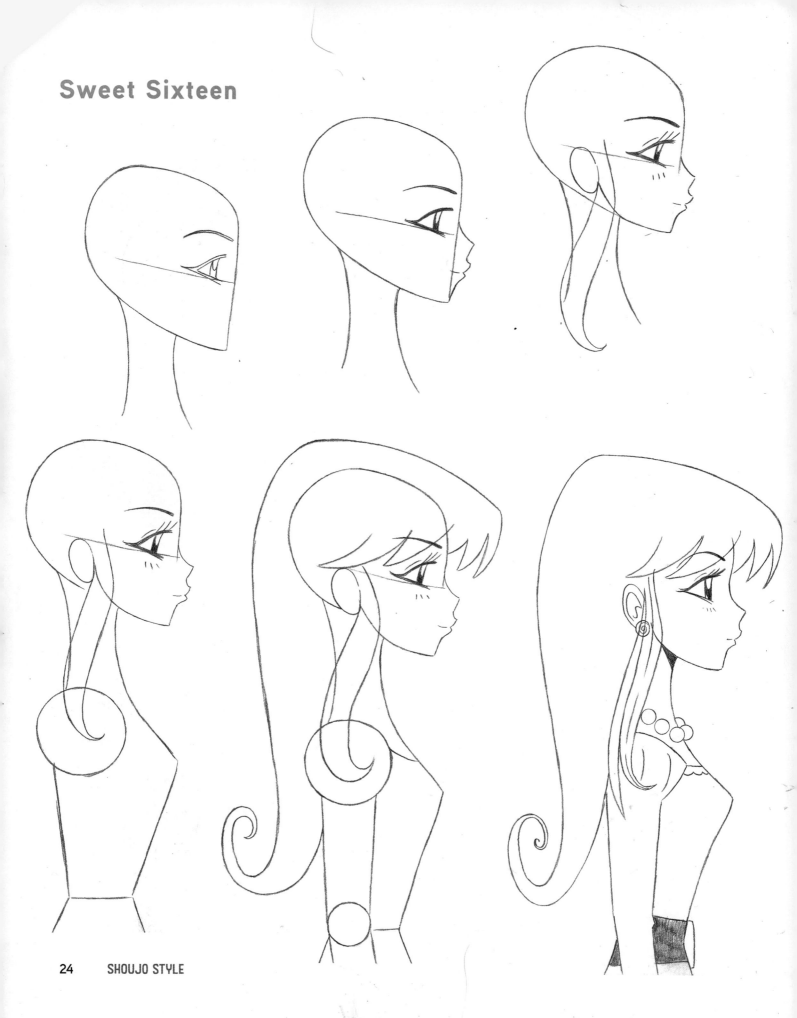

Wink! Wink!

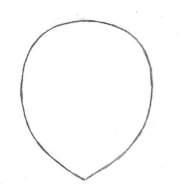

Wide-Eyed Boy

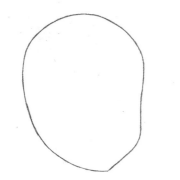

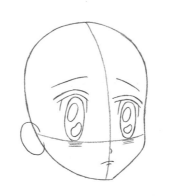

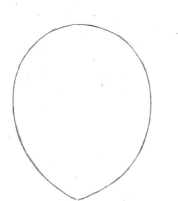

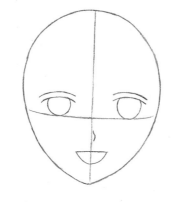

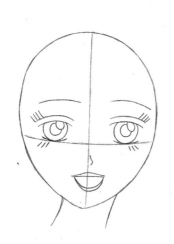

Happy Birthday!

High School Freshman

Winter Cheer

A Case of the Giggles!

J-Pop Fan

Perfect Pigtails

Bright-Eyed Betsy

Younger Brother

Shortstop

Glamorous Gal

Daydreaming Dave

Happy School Girl

Secret Smile

Pretty Profile

Princess with Tiara

Wide Eyes

Urban Chic

Silly Thought

Sweet Smile

School Boy

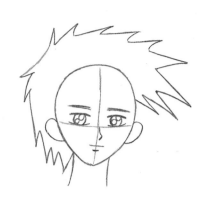

The Clique Queen

Friendly Teenager

Japanese School Uniform

Sushi Chef

Gentle Girl

SHOUJO STYLE

Dazzling Eyes

High Diver

Fun in the Sun

Pretty Maid

Tea Ceremony

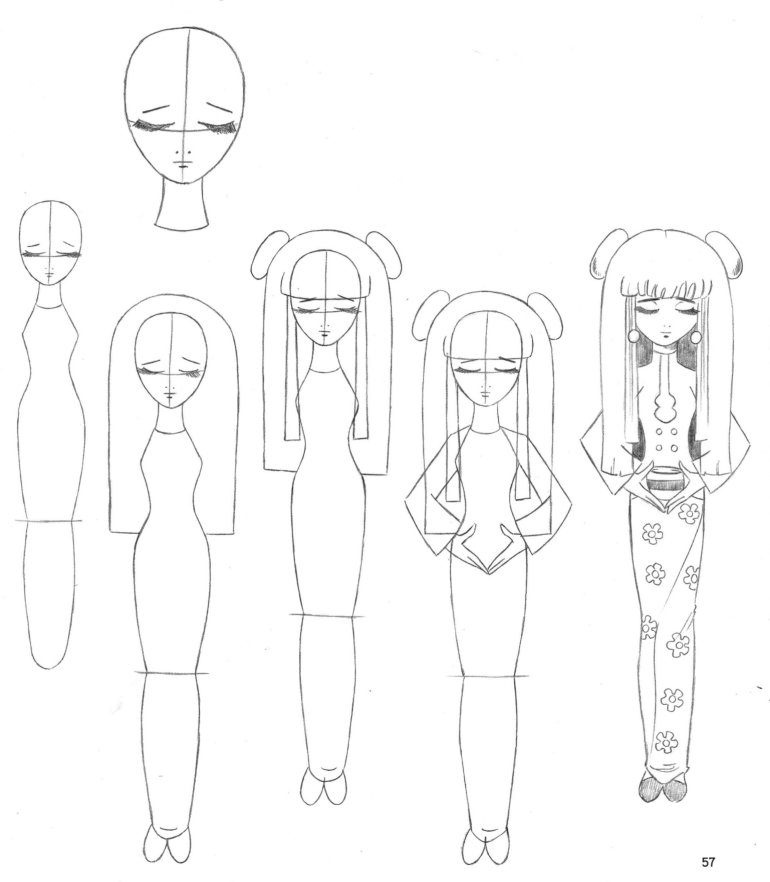

Can I Keep Him?

Kimono Girl

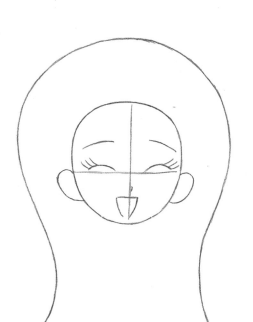

59

More Sushi Fun

School's Out!

Designer Cool

Stepping Out

School Spirit

Honor Student

MAGiCAL GiRLS

Magical girls are battle warriors, and they also happen to be some of the most popular heroes in all of manga. In a swirl of magic, they transform themselves from ordinary schoolgirls into beautiful fighting fantasy figures. Many possess special talents and powers, which they use to protect their friends from the forces of darkness.

Flying Pose

Power from the Wand

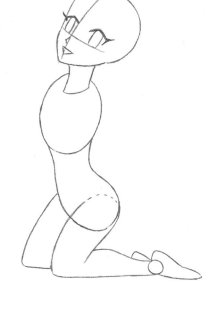
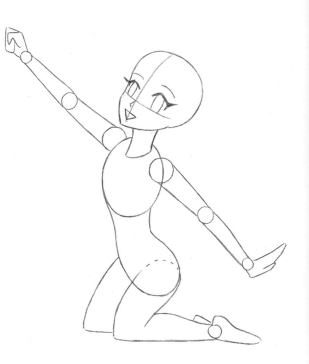

Watchful

Transforming

Stirring Power

Preparing for Battle

CAT GiRLS

Cat girls are cute half-human, half-animal hybrids.
Some are more human, others more feline—it's
completely up to you! Most cat girls have cat ears
and a tail, but you can make them more cat-like by
adding a cat nose and mouth, whiskers, and paws.

Pretty Cat Girl

Cat Girl Cutie

Feline Fashionista

Attractive Anthro

Glamour Puss

BiSHOUNEN STYLE

Bishounen (pronounced "bee-shown-nan") are the handsome teen guys who shoujo girls have crushes on, in popular manga graphic novels. Bishounen characters can be moody, aloof, and self-absorbed—in other words, typical teenage boys! Unlike shoujo boys, however, who have rounded faces and large eyes, bishounen boys are lanky and drawn with angular faces, giving them a more mature, idealized look. They're tall, with sleek eyes and long, thin noses.

Mr. Self-Confident

Mr. Moody

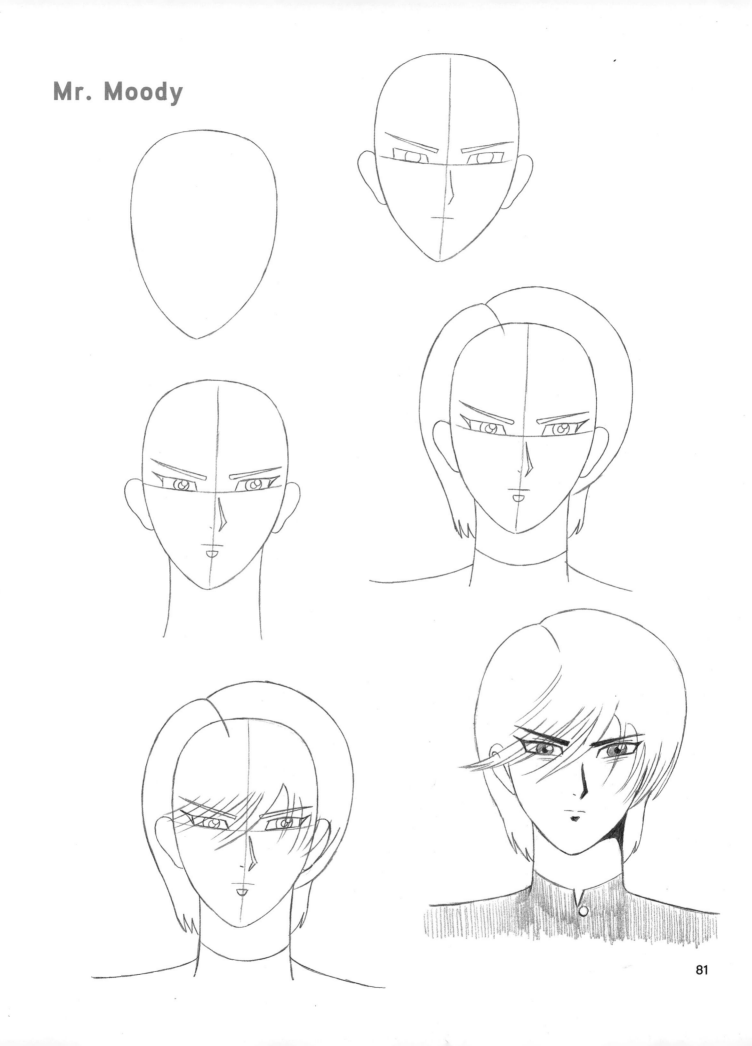

The Boyfriend

Very, Very Evil

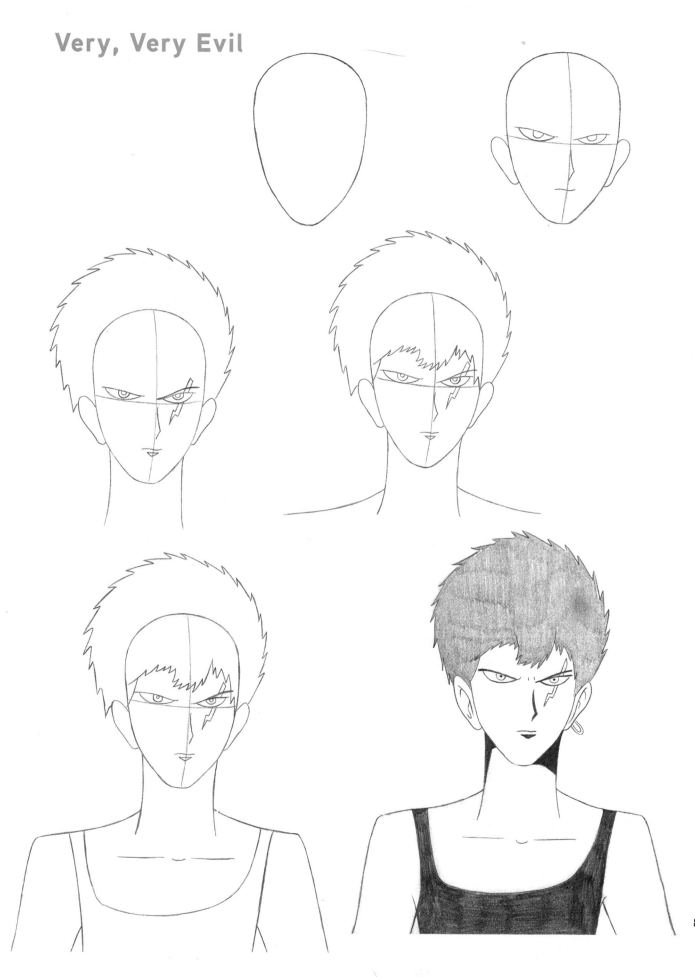

Serious Moment

Maniac Grin

Intense Look

BISHOUNEN STYLE

Sinister Smile

Love-Struck

Junior Prom Tom

Cool Jacket

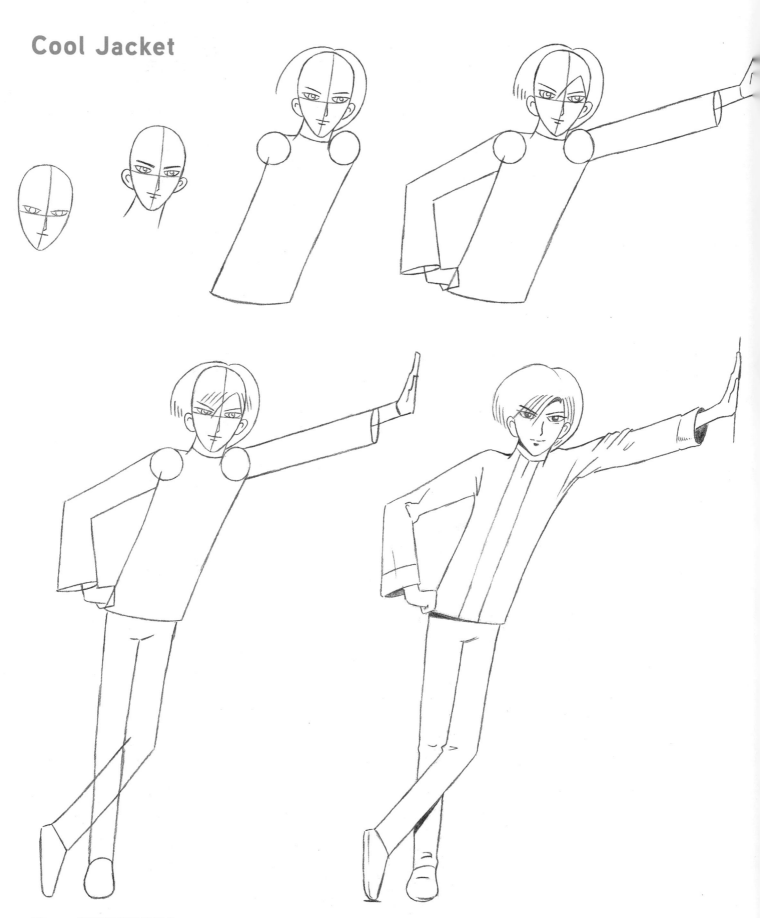

Casual Pose

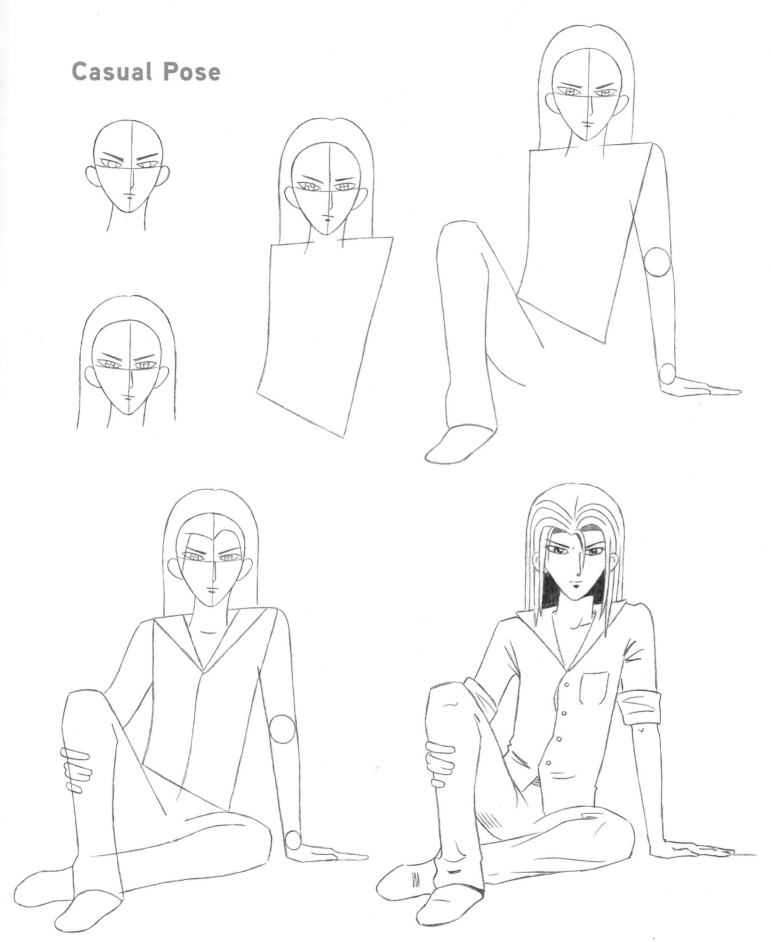

Antihero

Running

SHOUNEN STYLE

This action-packed style, pronounced "show-nan," is all about exciting action characters. Whether they are doing dynamic moves or just standing around, they should look the part of an action figure. No glamour gals or boyfriend types here. They should have a bit of an edgy look—usually spiky hair for guys, and the look of a tigress, ready to fight, for gals. No school uniforms but instead battle-ready costumes!

Karate Kicker!

Ready for Anything!

Super-Spiked Hair

Dojo Boy

Samurai Warrior

Never Give Up!

Double-Crosser

Ninja Girl

Secret Agent

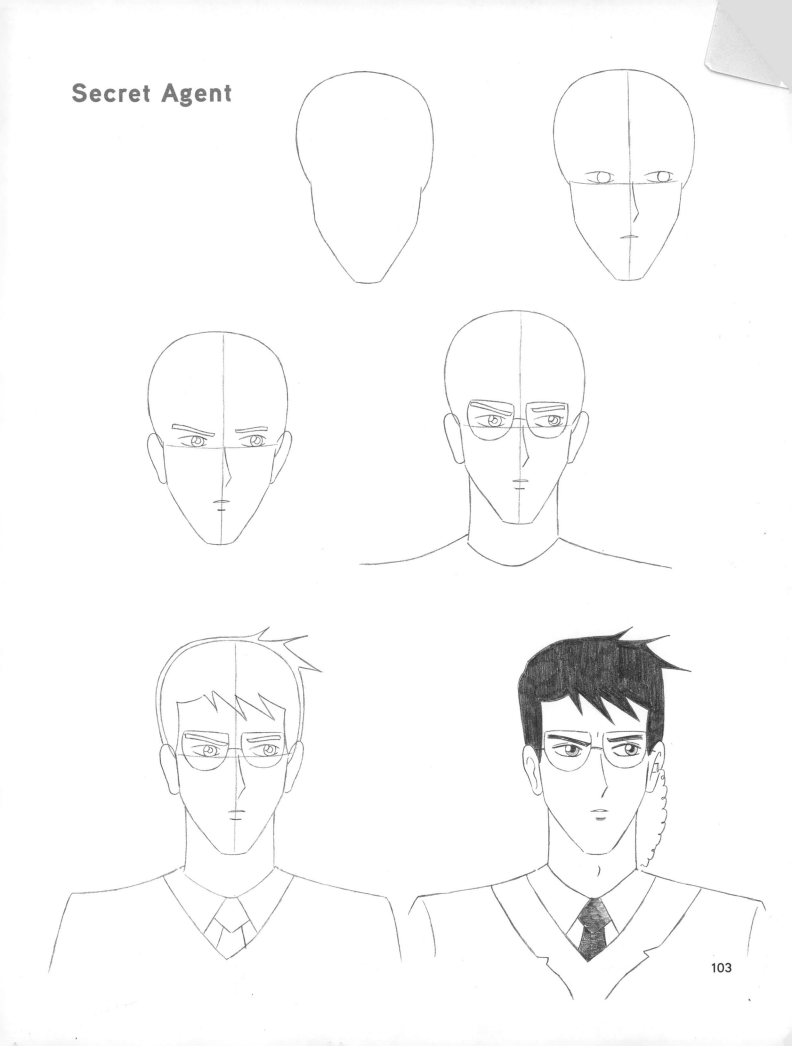

CHiBiS, CREATURES, AND MANGA ANiMALS

Everything in this chapter is mini! Tiny people, min-imonsters, and pint-sized animal friends. Chibis, the hilarious miniature people that add comic relief in so many manga graphic novels, have huge heads stuck on top of short, chubby bodies, which makes them incredibly adorable! Chibis are supercuties!

Most manga monsters are round and cuddly—a few of them are strange and otherworldly, but they're never truly scary. Manga animals are either adorable or goofy. Smaller animals are the most fun, and easiest, to draw.

Frightened Little Chibi

Happy Chibi

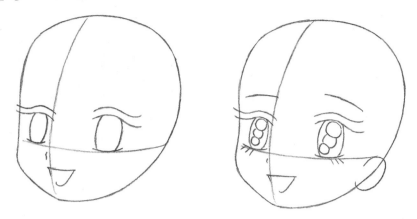

Chibi Sword Fighter

Chibi Chef

Chibi Softball Player

Horn Puff

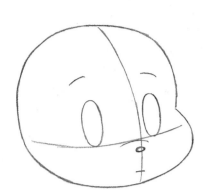

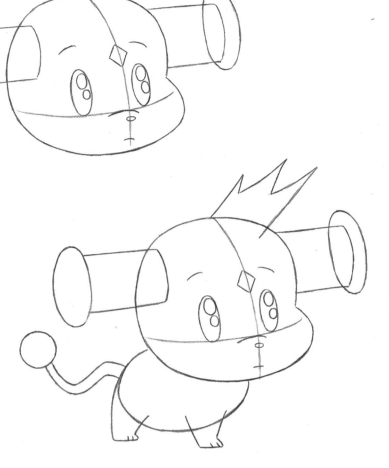

Dark Crab

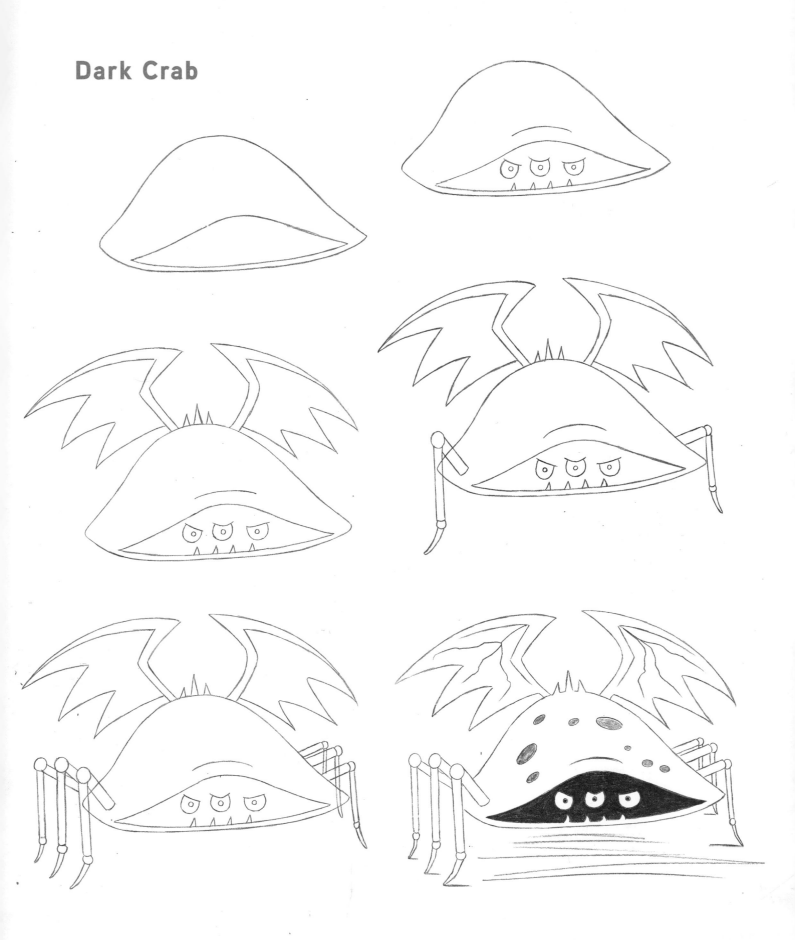

Monster Porker

Thing Z

Dino Chub

Tubbysaurus

Pudgerfly

Fluffer Bunny

Funky Monkey

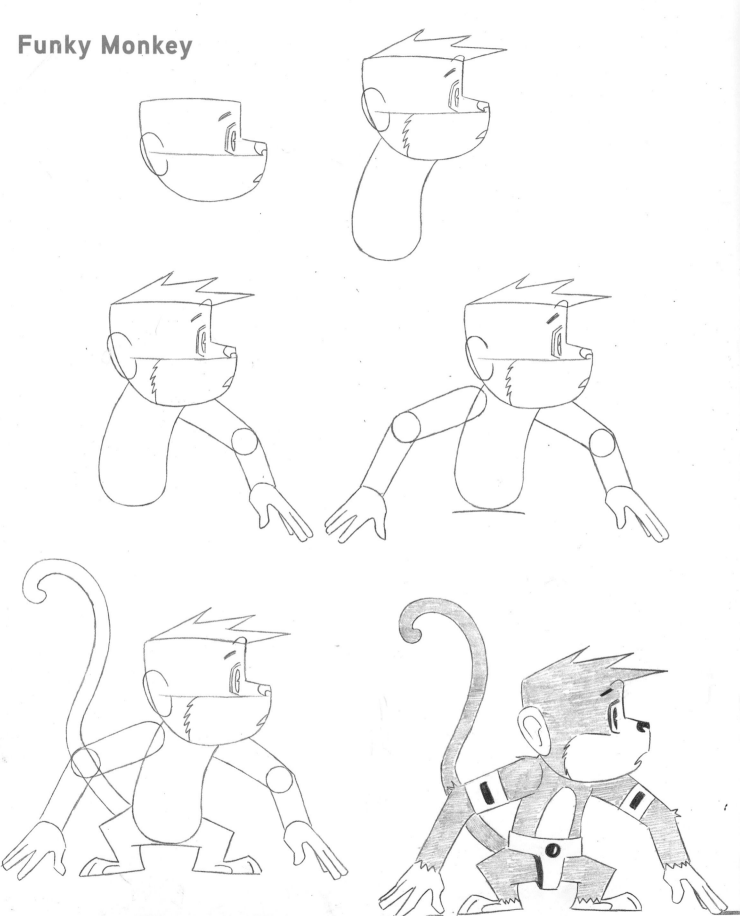

Dr. Catz

FANTASY AND SCi-Fi CHARACTERS

Peasant-like costumes, pointed ears, almond-shaped eyes, and upturned noses turn regular characters into elves and faerie folk. For sci-fi characters, cool costumes and cutting-edge designs create a futuristic look. Some outer-space gear, such as earpieces, belts, and weapons, are also good added touches.

Faerie Archer

Young Explorer

FANTASY AND SCi-Fi CHARACTERS

Beautiful Mermaid

Boy Wizard

Faerie Girl

Adventure Boy

Sci-Fi Attacker

Mecha Commander

Starship Cop

Grieving Starship Soldier

Mars Captain

Android Girl

Futuristic Girl

Lady Scientist

Rookie Pilot

GOTH AND OCCULT CHARACTERS

Goth and occult-style characters are usually drawn with dark eyes and darkened eyelashes and wear lots of black. Sometimes they are just plain evil—like vampires and witches. But even the goth characters without supernatural powers have a dark charm.

Goth Girl

Dashing Vampire

Urban Goth

Cute Witch

Bat Trainer

Queen of Darkness

Goth Guy